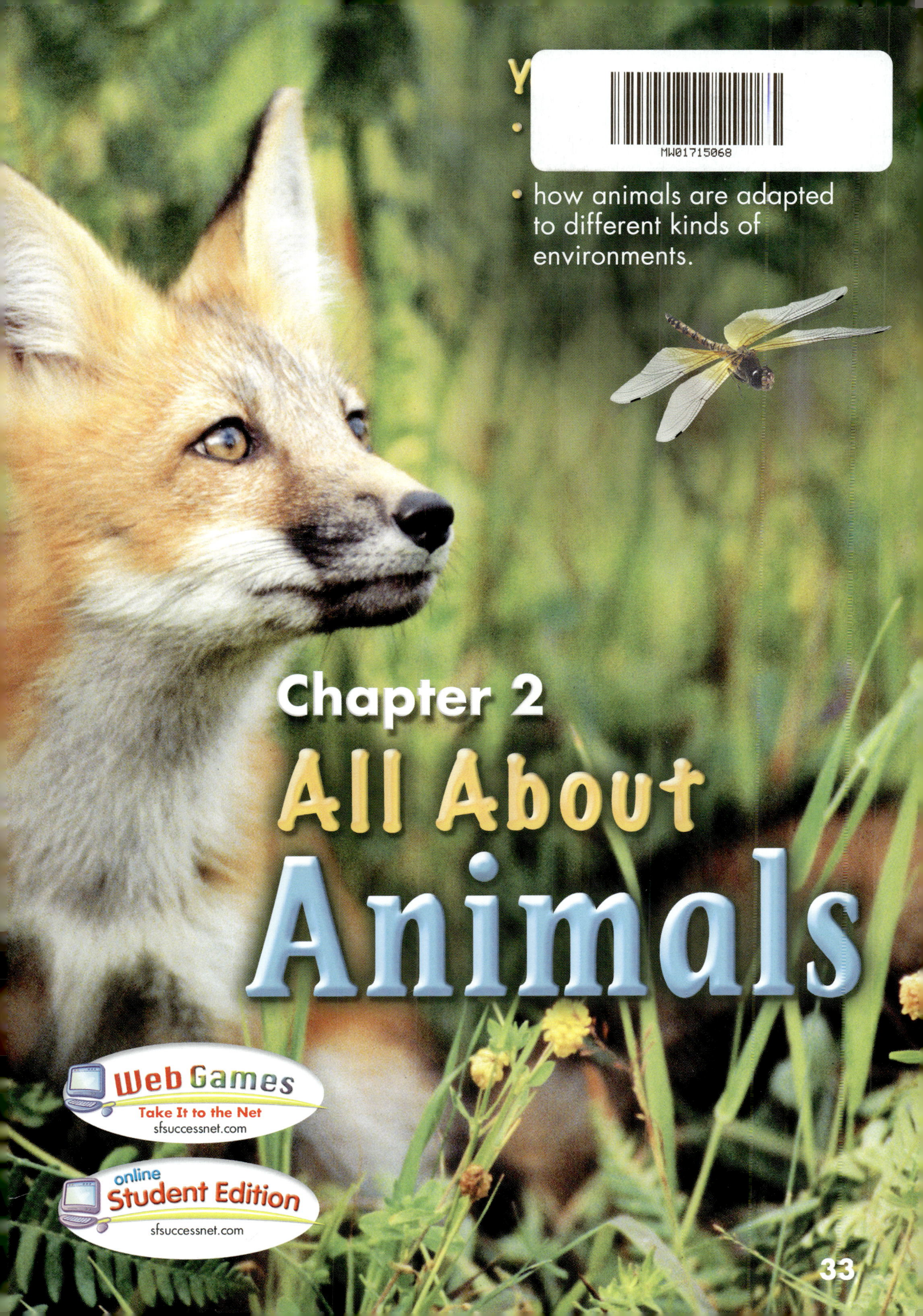

-
- how animals are adapted to different kinds of environments.

Chapter 2
All About Animals

Web Games
Take It to the Net
sfsuccessnet.com

online Student Edition
sfsuccessnet.com

Build Background

How are animals different from each other?

Chapter 2 Vocabulary

mammal page 40

bird page 40

fish page 40

reptile page 41

amphibian page 41

camouflage page 42

gills page 46

insect page 52

Lab zone

Directed Inquiry

Explore How are worms and snakes alike and different?

Materials

short tape

long tape

7 cotton squares

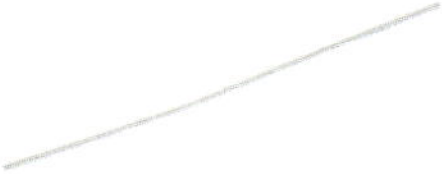
pipe cleaner

14 pieces of pasta

What to Do

Make models of a worm and a snake.

Worm

1. Roll up.
   Pinch the ends.

Snake

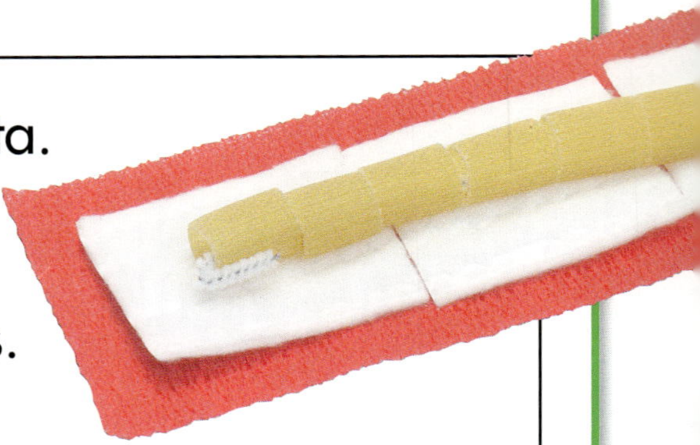

2. String the pasta.
3. Roll up.
   Pinch the ends.

Process Skills

Models show how animals are alike and different.

Explain Your Results

Feel the **models**. Tell about them.

How to Read Science

Reading Skills

Alike and Different

Alike means how things are the same.
Different means how things are not the same.

Science Article

Worms and Snakes

Worms are long and thin. Worms do not have backbones. Worms use their bodies to crawl. Snakes are long and thin. Snakes have backbones. Snakes use their bodies to crawl.

Apply It!

Tell how a worm and a snake are alike and different. Use your **models** to help you.

Alike	Different

You Are There

What Has Backbones?

Sung to the tune of "There's a Hole In The Bucket"
Lyrics by Gerri Brioso & Richard Freitas/The Dovetail Group, Inc.

There are animals with backbones,
Like mammals.
Yes, mammals.
Dogs and cats,
Skunks and chipmunks,
All have backbones.

Lesson 1

What are some animals with backbones?

There are many different kinds of animals. One main group of animals has backbones.

Bones help give an animal shape. Bones can help an animal move. Bones can help protect some body parts of animals.

A skunk has a backbone.

Animals with Backbones

Mammals are animals with backbones.
A mammal usually has hair or fur on its body.
Young mammals get milk from their mother.
Dogs and cats are two kinds of mammals.
The chipmunk in the picture is a mammal.

Birds are animals with backbones. Birds have feathers and wings. Birds hatch from eggs.

Fish are animals with backbones. Fish live in water. Most fish are covered with scales. Fish have fins. Most fish hatch from eggs.

Reptiles are animals with backbones. Most reptiles have dry skin. Scales cover and protect a reptile's body. Some reptiles hatch from eggs. Snakes and turtles are two kinds of reptiles.

Amphibians are animals with backbones. Amphibians live part of their life in the water and part of their life on land. Most amphibians have smooth, wet skin. Amphibians hatch from eggs. Frogs and toads are amphibians.

Lesson Checkpoint

1. Which kinds of animals have backbones and scales?
2. How are an amphibian and a reptile **alike** and **different?**

reptile

amphibian

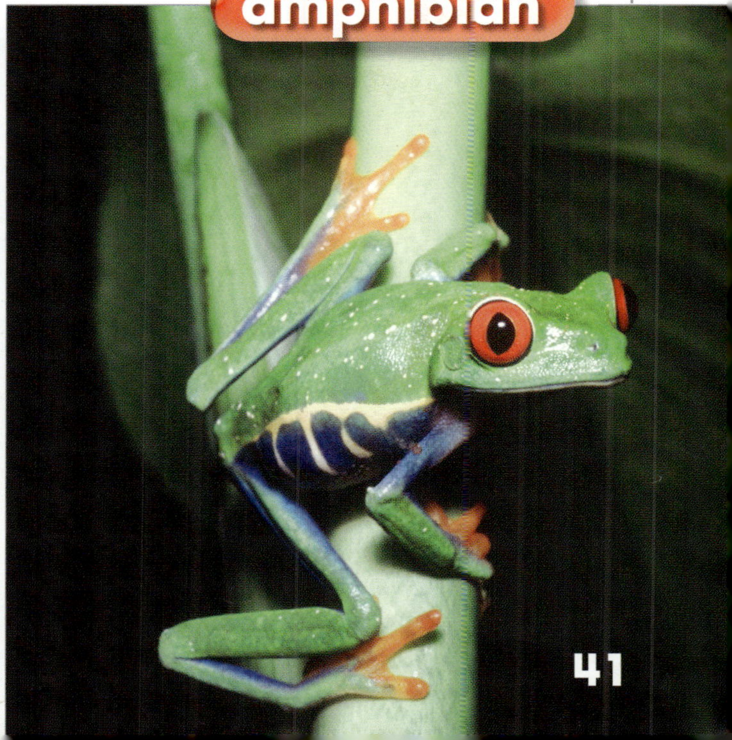

Lesson 2

What are some ways mammals are adapted?

Mammals live almost everywhere in the world. Like plants, mammals have adapted to live in their environment. An animal's environment is all the living and nonliving things around it.

Like many animals, mule deer are adapted to their environment by camouflage. **Camouflage** is a color or shape that makes a plant or animal hard to see.

The mule deer's fur is brown in summer.

In winter, the mule deer's fur turns color. The deer is harder to see in the snow.

A flying squirrel is adapted to glide from tree to tree.

A chipmunk sleeps for part of the winter.

Some animals are adapted to act in ways that help them live. Chipmunks store some of the food they find in the summer. They sleep for part of the winter. Chipmunks eat some of the food they store every time they wake up.

✓ Lesson Checkpoint

1. How does a mule deer's fur change in winter?
2. **Art in Science** Draw a picture of a mammal that you have seen.

Lesson 3

What are some ways birds are adapted?

Many birds are adapted to fly. Their wings and feathers help them fly.

This bird is called a nightjar.

This nightjar lives in the forest. Its feathers look like the forest floor. This camouflage helps the bird hide from animals that might eat it.

Hmmm!

A hummingbird's beak is adapted to help it get food. A hummingbird uses its beak to sip liquid from flowers.

Most penguins live where it is very cold.

A penguin's top feathers are waterproof. These feathers help keep the penguin dry. Tiny feathers below the top feathers trap air. The trapped air helps keep the penguin warm.

Penguins do not fly. Their wings are adapted for swimming.

✓ Lesson Checkpoint

1. How does camouflage protect the nightjar?
2. How are hummingbirds and penguins **alike?** How are they **different?**

Lesson 4

What are some ways fish are adapted?

Fish are adapted to life in the water. Fish have gills. **Gills** are body parts that help fish get oxygen from the water. Fish have fins to help them swim.

This porcupine fish is adapted to protect itself. The porcupine fish can make itself big. Sharp spikes stick out from its body when it is big.

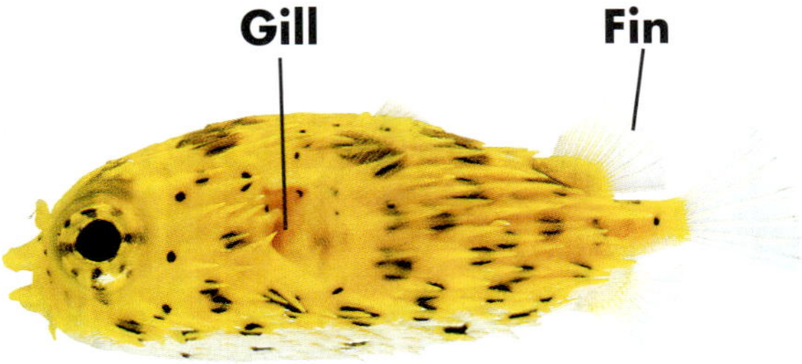

This tiny porcupine fish can become very big.

Changing shape protects the porcupine fish.

Many catfish live in lakes and rivers. Catfish can swim deep in the water where it is dark. Catfish have feelers that look like whiskers. Feelers help catfish find food.

Long feelers help a catfish find food.

This stingray uses the sharp spike on its tail to protect itself.

✓ Lesson Checkpoint

1. How do porcupine fish protect themselves?
2. **Math in Science** Some catfish are only 10 centimeters long. Use a ruler. Draw a line 10 centimeters long. Find something in your classroom that is the same length.

Lesson 5

What are some ways reptiles are adapted?

Reptiles are adapted to changes in air temperature. A reptile's body is cold when the air is cold. A reptile's body is warm when the air is warm. Reptiles can move quickly when they are warm.

Zap!

A chameleon has a long tongue. The chameleon has a sticky ball at the end of its tongue. Food sticks to this ball.

Open wide!

This snake's mouth is adapted to open very wide. This snake can swallow its food whole.

A desert iguana is adapted to live in the hot, sunny desert. Dark colors get hot in the sun. Light colors stay cooler in the sun. The light skin helps the desert iguana keep cool.

desert iguana

✓ Lesson Checkpoint

1. How is a desert iguana adapted to live in its environment?
2. **Writing in Science** Tell one way some snakes are adapted to get food.

Lesson 6

What are some ways amphibians are adapted?

Most amphibians begin their life in the water. Many amphibians move to the land when they are grown. Frogs are amphibians. Frogs often live near water. Smooth, wet skin helps frogs live in moist environments.

These tree frogs have bright red eyes. Other animals want to eat the frogs. The frogs' eyes help scare these animals away.

Toads are amphibians. Toads begin their life in water. Toads move to the land when they are grown. Toads dig deep into the ground when it is very hot. They look for food at night.

Most toads have dry, rough skin.

✓ Lesson Checkpoint

1. Name one way a toad and a frog are different.
2. **Writing in Science** Tell how bright red eyes can help a tree frog.

Lesson 7

What are some animals without backbones?

One main group of animals has backbones. Another main group of animals does not have backbones. Most kinds of animals do not have bones.

Insects are animals that do not have bones. Insects have three body parts. The body parts are the head, the thorax, and the abdomen. Insects have six legs. Antennae help some insects feel, smell, hear, and taste.

This insect is called a walking stick. Camouflage makes the insect hard to see on a plant.

Some kinds of honeypot ants are adapted to store water and food in their abdomens.

A diving beetle's legs are adapted for swimming. A diving beetle has many hairs on its legs. The hairy legs help the beetle move through the water.

1. **Checkpoint** How is the diving beetle adapted to life in water?
2. **Technology in Science** Tell about inventions that help people move in water.

Other Animals Without Backbones

An octopus lives in the ocean. An octopus is an animal without a backbone.

An octopus is adapted to find and catch food. An octopus has good eyesight. Its eyesight helps it find food. The suction cups on its arms help the octopus hold its food.

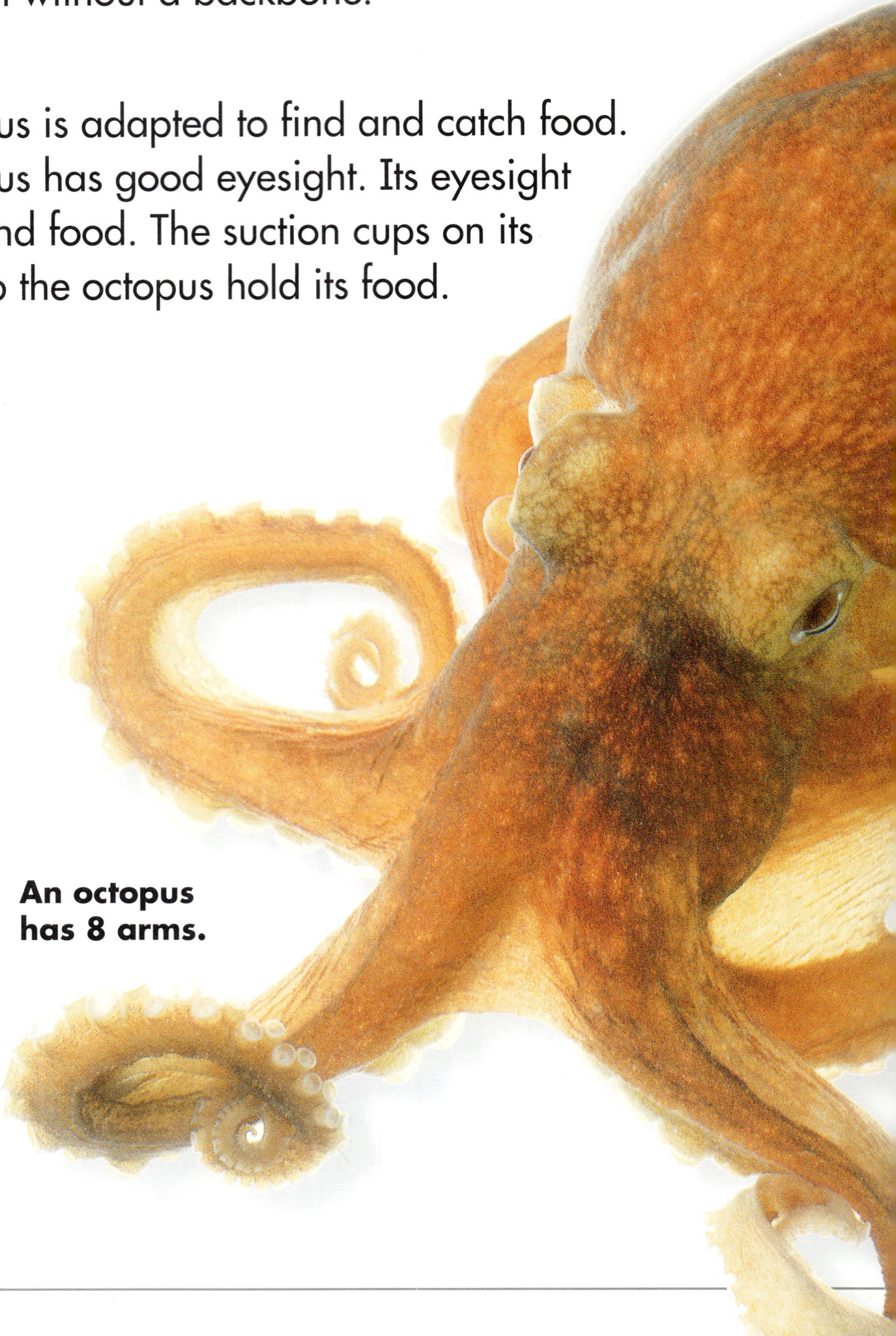

An octopus has 8 arms.

Spiders are animals without backbones. Spiders have eight legs. Spiders are adapted to spin webs. The webs trap insects that spiders eat.

This spider builds a web to trap insects.

✓ Lesson Checkpoint

1. Tell how the octopus is adapted to find food.
2. **Math** in Science A spider has 8 legs. How many legs will 2 spiders have in all? Write a number sentence to show your answer.

Lab zone

Guided Inquiry

Investigate How can an octopus use its arms?

An octopus has suction cups on its 8 arms. It can use its arms to pick things up. Billye the octopus uses its arms to solve a problem. Billye can open a jar to get a fish inside.

Materials

scissors

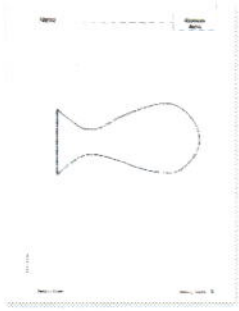

fish

jar

8 suction cups

What to Do

1. Cut out the fish.

2. Put the fish in the jar. **Predict** how many suction cups you will need to open a jar.

Process Skills

When you share your ideas, you **communicate** with your classmates.

More Lab zone Activities Take It to the Net sfsuccessnet.com

3. Work with your group. Take turns. Try to open the jar with suction cups. Where should you put them?

4. How many suction cups did you predict? How many did you use?

How many suction cups will open a jar?								
Predict								
Test								
	1	2	3	4	5	6	7	8

Number of Suction Cups

Explain Your Results

Communicate Tell how you used the suction cups.

Go Further

What other problems can you solve using suction cups? Try to solve the problems!

Sorting Animals

Sort these animals into 2 groups. One group has animals with backbones. Count the number of animals with backbones. The other group has animals without backbones. Count the number of animals without backbones.

Make a graph like this one. Color in your graph to show the number of animals in each group.

Animal Groups

Animals with backbones									
Animals without backbones									
	0 1	2	3	4	5	6	7	8	9

Number of Animals

1. Which group has the most animals?
2. Which group has the fewest animals?

snake

porcupine fish

Lab zone Take-Home Activity

Take a nature walk. List all of the animals you see. Sort the animals into groups.

Chapter 2 Review and Test Prep

Vocabulary

Which picture goes with each word?

1. insect
2. mammal
3. amphibian
4. fish
5. bird
6. reptile

A

B

C

D

E

F

What did you learn?

7. How do fish use gills?
8. How does camouflage help protect animals?
9. Name 2 kinds of animals with backbones. Name 2 kinds of animals without backbones.

Process Skills

10. **Communicate** Choose an animal in this chapter. Tell one way the animal is adapted to its environment.

Alike and Different

11. Tell how a spider and an insect are **alike and different.**

Alike	Different

Test Prep

Fill in the circle next to the correct answer.

12. Which kind of animal has feathers and wings?

Ⓐ fish
Ⓑ bird
Ⓒ mammal
Ⓓ amphibian

13. **Writing in Science** Choose an animal. Tell how the animal is adapted to its environment.

Life Along the Ice

Scientists working with NASA study ways that animals survive in different environments. Many penguins live in the ocean near Antarctica. Antarctica is very cold. It is covered with ice and snow.

Most of the ocean water near Antarctica is full of ice. The wind blows holes in some places in the ice. Plants called algae can grow in the holes in the ice. Tiny animals called krill eat the algae. Penguins that live near the water eat krill.

Krill

Scientists working with NASA use satellites to study the ocean. The satellites are in space. The satellites send information about the ocean back to Earth. Scientists have learned that when there is more algae, there are more krill. When there are more krill, there are more penguins. When there are fewer krill, there are fewer penguins.

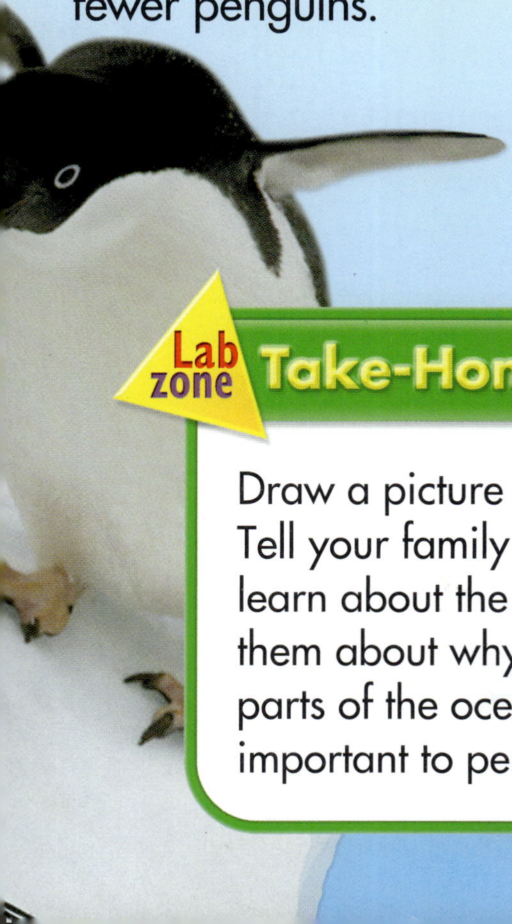

Lab zone Take-Home Activity

Draw a picture of a penguin. Tell your family how scientists learn about the ocean. Tell them about why the warmer parts of the ocean are important to penguins.

Career

Wildlife Rehabilitator

Read Together

What happens when animals that live in forests or oceans are hurt? Are there ways people can help?

Wildlife rehabilitators are people that help hurt or sick animals. They know what animals need to live in their environment. A wildlife rehabilitator can even teach young animals how to hunt for food.

Wildlife rehabilitators know that it is important that animals get the care they need to survive.

A wildlife rehabilitator saved this sea turtle.

Lab zone Take-Home Activity

Write about what it would be like to be a wildlife rehabilitator. What kinds of animals would you like to help?